THE PROFESSIONAL
NURSE

MARKET
YOURSELF

FOR SUCCESSFUL
RESULTS

Dr. Pamela C. Smith

Michele A. Mazurowski

The Professional Nurse
Market Yourself For Successful Results

First Printing, 2014

ISBN-13: 978-1505469813
ISBN-10: 1505469813

Class Act
Consulting and Professional Development, LLC

Is a trademark of Class Act Consulting and Professional Development

Table of Contents

Dedication

This book is dedicated to Rita F. D'Aoust, PhD, ANP-BC, CNE, FAANP, FNAP; Craig R. Sellers, PhD, RN, ANP-BC, GNP-BC, FAANP; and Andrew F. Wall, PhD for their wisdom, scholarship, and continuous support of personal and professional development.

About the Authors

Dr. Pamela C. Smith has more than thirty-five years of professional experience in healthcare and education. She has held a variety of entrepreneurial and innovative positions in leadership, management, practice and academics; serving as a provider, an educator, a leader, a mentor and a consultant. For the complete bio, see page 16.

Michele A. Mazurowski has more than thirty-five years of experience in the legal field. Michele realized early in her career that professional image and presentation are key to success. Flawless in her presentation, with meticulous attention to detail, she has personally shopped and advised individuals working in the corporate and legal fields on how to dress for success. Michele believes that dressing for success does not have to be costly, that one can obtain a professional wardrobe and create a certain image on a budget.

With a background in Journalism and English literature, Michele has mentored and tutored numerous individuals with their writing, communication, and research skills which led to successful results.

For many years, Michele has served as Treasurer for several local committees and organizations implementing strong moral and ethical values. Over the course of Michele's legal career, she has exhibited exemplary customer service and organizational skills that have proven instrumental in building and retaining strong business relationships necessary for innovation and growth.

For more information or to contact the authors, please visit www.classactdevelopment.com

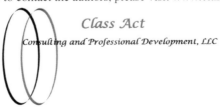

iii

Preface

As nurses are challenged to explore, lead, and create a strategic vision for growth and sustainability, they must adapt to a modern environment wherein they become comfortable with self-promotion. One way to achieve this state of self-promotion is to create a Professional Development Toolkit. The Professional Development Toolkit contains twenty components that will help nurses better articulate their strengths, skills, talents and abilities. These components will help guide them as they navigate their career path and find their "best fit" to meet workforce demands. Utilizing the components in the Professional Development Toolkit will promote ongoing professional and personal development, at all levels, and assist with marketing strategies and techniques to achieve successful results.

Whether you are an aspiring nurse currently enrolled in a nursing program, or a staff nurse, a nurse manager or leader, or a nurse executive; considering a job promotion, retaining a current position, or entering the workforce; professional and personal development is lifelong and necessary for success and sustainability as you embark on your career journey. Nurses at all levels need to be able to articulate their strengths, skills, talents and abilities for successful results, understanding that ongoing professional and personal development is imperative in today's ever changing and evolving healthcare environment. This commitment to professional and personal development is also clearly stated in the American Nurses Association (ANA) Code of Ethics for Nurses Provision 5, whereas "The nurse owes the same duties to self as to others, including the responsibility to preserve integrity and safety, to maintain competence, and to continue personal and professional growth (2010, p. 9).

Nursing, one of the largest professions in the United States (US), with over 3 million nurses in total, and 84.8% currently employed in nursing (American Association of Colleges of Nursing [AACN], 2011), practice across a variety of settings which include but are not limited to; hospitals, school-based and community health centers, academia and many other not-for-profit and for-profit organizations. Currently, nurses are expected to navigate a remarkably complex and fast-paced healthcare environment, often facing situations requiring decisions that have an economic, social, political, and professional impact.

The downturn in the US economy in 2008 added an additional challenge for individual nurses and the profession of nursing. The availability of nursing positions, once plentiful, have become more specialized and even limited in certain geographic areas within the US, where there are many applicants for fewer positions. In addition, 30% - 50% of new nurses entering the profession are electing to change positions or leave the profession altogether within the first two to three years of practice (Chambers, 2010; MacKusick & Minick, 2010). "The real cost of replacing a medical/surgical nurse is $42,000 and $64,000 for a specialty nurse. Kaiser Permanente places an even higher price tag on nurse turnover — $47,403 for a medical/surgical nurse and $85,197 for a specialty nurse" (Alter Group, 2011). In addition, there are other hidden costs that affect the quality and safety of patient care such as increased contingent staff costs, increased workload, increased absenteeism and increased patient errors that take a toll on other members of the healthcare team. Recruiting and retaining top nursing talent is essential for creating a healthy, safe, quality, and economical healthcare environment. Securing a nursing position is not a guarantee in today's economy, much less securing a nursing position that is a good fit. Finding the best fit is crucial for both the nurse and the organization to create a win-win situation.

With the implementation of the Patient Protection and Affordable Health Care and Education Reconciliation Act (PPACA) (2010), along with other new regulations and standards, nurses will be called upon to help meet the demand and fill the void for healthcare services across practice and educational settings. The recent game-changing document released by the Institute of Medicine (IOM) in 2011, *The Future of Nursing: Leading Change, Advancing Health*, addresses four key messages and eight recommendations for nurses to become partners and leaders in shaping the direction, and improving healthcare in the United States (US). The authors identify and recommend strategies necessary for nurses to meet current and future challenges. Nurses need to tap into their entrepreneurial and innovative spirit and recognize opportunities to explore, lead, and create a strategic vision for growth and sustainability (IOM, 2011).

As we move forward in the 21st century with limited resources, leaders and decision makers in healthcare organizations and systems will need to create ways to address the many healthcare challenges. Historically, the focus of education and training for nurses has been on caring for patients and their families with little emphasis on self-promotion, and the ability to articulate the value that nurses bring to all facets of the healthcare environment.

Currently, nurses have a unique opportunity to firmly establish and sustain their position within the ever changing healthcare environment. If nurses are going to play key roles as leaders and team members to meet the challenges in this reformed healthcare environment, they must be able to articulate and demonstrate the value they contribute. Nurses must be aware and comfortable with their strengths, skills, talents and abilities, as well as what differentiates them from other nurses and other healthcare professionals when competing for positions. Introduction to self promotion should begin in nursing school and continue throughout the nurse's career.

Professional Development Toolkit Model

The Professional Development Toolkit is designed with the nurse at the center core. The circle in the model represents infinity, without a beginning or end, as well as without sides or corners. The nurse is the constant focus, whereas the information and content within the twenty (20) components of the toolkit are always evolving and changing as the nurse progresses throughout their career.

Getting Started

You have chosen a career in nursing, one of the biggest and greatest decisions you have ever made. In 2013, nursing was once again rated as the most trusted profession based on honesty and ethical standards, according to a Gallup survey (Advance Healthcare Network for Nurses, 2014). Achieving your nursing degree has not only provided you entry into the most trusted profession (Gallup, 2014), but it has opened the doors of endless possibilities and options. There are more than 100 specialty areas in nursing. Some of the more traditional roles for nursing practice include but are not limited to the areas of: Medical-Surgical, Critical Care, Emergency, Ambulatory Care/Medical Office, Occupational Health, Oncology, Dialysis, Operating Room/Post Anesthesia Care Unit, Orthopaedics, Pediatrics, Geriatrics/Long-Term Care, Community and/or Public Health, Women's Health, Psychiatric-Mental Health.

More non-traditional nursing roles to consider include, but are not limited to, Nurse Entrepreneur, Nurse Executive (Chief Nursing Officer, Chief Executive Officer, Chief Operating Officer, Chief Quality Officer, etc), Registered Nurse First Assistant (RNFA), Legal Nurse Consultant, Nurse Legislator, Forensic Nurse Examiner, Sexual Assault Nurse Examiner (SANE), Case Management Nurse, Nursing Professional Development Specialist (formerly known as Nurse Educator of Staff Development Nurse), Certified Nurse Anesthetist, Certified Nurse Mid-Wife, Nurse Practitioner, Disaster Management Nurse, Flight Nurse, Health Promotion Specialist, Nurse Specialist in Travel and Tropical Medicine, Wound/Ostomy/Continence Nurse Specialist, Clinical Trials Research Nurse, Infection Control Nurse Specialist and many more.

While there is a plethora of information available regarding nurses and the nursing profession, websites such as Johnson & Johnson Discover Nursing - Campaign for Nursing, American Nurses Credentialing Center (ANCC), American Nurses Association, Nursing World, are just a few of the wonderful resources available. Given the many possibilities in nursing, there is plenty of opportunity to stay within the profession, and achieve job satisfaction in your current or future nursing role (s) as you proceed throughout your career.

Getting started, you first need to identify your perfect job. This task can be accomplished through thoughtful consideration and by putting your thoughts in writing. This provides an opportunity for you to develop your thoughts further. You can put your thoughts in writing now or at a later date. In addition, writing your perfect job helps you to focus on what is most important to you as well as what is negotiable and non-negotiable. You must ask yourself this question, *"What is my perfect job/role in nursing?"* This question is ongoing and the answer will change over time.

Tips:

When writing your perfect job, be honest and realistic. This is your document and you do not need to share it with anyone. Some example questions you may want to consider when writing your perfect job may include:

- Where do I see myself working? (Think about the physical setting such as a major medical center, smaller community hospital, outpatient clinic, private physician's office, school, law office, etc.)
- What hours can I work? Are you able to work evenings and/or nights? Can you work 8, 10, 12 hour shifts, weekends and holidays? (If you have commitments at home with little to no flexibility, will you be able to work overtime or off shifts if required?)
- How much money do I need to make to afford the lifestyle I desire?
- How do I want to dress for work everyday?
- Where do I see myself in 1 year, 3 years, 5 years?
- Am I planning on pursuing a higher degree in the future?
- Do I need a position that will offer me autonomy? Status?
- Do I need benefits, and if so, which ones?
- How far away from home am I willing to travel?

Exercise:

Write your perfect job. This does not need to be a daunting endeavor. Think of it this way, the good fairy has offered to grant you your perfect job, and there are no limitations. Itemize on paper what constitutes your perfect job in relationship to location, job duties, financials, hours per work week, and anything else that matters to you. More information to assist you with this endeavor will be covered in future chapters within this book.

Chapter 1: The Value of Business Cards

Now that you are thinking about your perfect job, do you have business cards that you can hand out? It has been said that 98% of all opportunity comes from networking. You never know when or where you are going to meet someone that could offer you, or connect you with a new opportunity. Business cards are an effective self-promotional networking and marketing tool. Providing your new contact(s) with a business card will increase your chances of being contacted in the future. It also serves as a tool that can be passed along to others who may be able to provide you with an opportunity.

Your business card serves as a first impression of yourself and/or your organization. When making the decision to utilize business cards, there are a few questions that must be answered. Do you currently have a business card(s)? Was it provided by a current employer? Should you give out an employer-provided business card to those you meet who could offer you a potential opportunity unrelated to your current employer? It is important to ask these questions before providing a business card, "Who am I representing and who will benefit from this potential new opportunity?" If the potential new opportunity or networking benefits the organization that provides your business cards, then it is appropriate to give out one of your employer-provided business cards. If the opportunity does not involve the organization that currently employs you, you will want to consider giving them your own personal business card. If you do not have a personal business card you can create your own using the tips listed below.

Once you have a business card(s) it is important to know the etiquette of giving and receiving business cards. It is not recommended to ask for or pass business cards out to everyone you meet. Rather, be thoughtful and selective with whom you choose to exchange information. When accepting a business card you should immediately review it and write on the back of the card any identifying information about the person or organization that you may need to access for future reference. If you are traveling abroad, or meeting with international healthcare contacts, it is important to research the business card etiquette for that particular country or culture.

Business cards are an accepted method of exchanging information for networking, as well as promoting yourself or your organization.

Information that should be included on a business card:
- Name and Credentials
- Title
- Logo and design are optional; if you decide on either one, make sure they are professional. If you are not sure, ask someone who specializes in professional development. It is best to adhere to the old adage that "less is more"
- Organization Name (optional)
- Contact Information
    - Address (optional)
    - Phone Number
    - E-mail address (Make sure it is professional. Avoid e-mail addresses like HottieRN@yahoo.com or pedsteddybearnurse@gmail.com)
- Organization Web Address
- Social Networking Sites

How to Obtain Business Cards
- Create Your Own (You can purchase blank business cards at your local office supply store). Make sure the brand of business cards has "clean edges," for a more professional look
- Printing Company
- Internet sites

Exercise:

Create your own personal business cards and keep them with you at all times. Opportunity is everywhere and you will be prepared.

Figure 1. Sample Simple Design

Figure 2. Sample Professional Design

Chapter 2: Professional Presentation

It has been said that you only have seven seconds to make a first impression when you meet someone for the first time, and non-verbal cues are four times more influential than verbal cues (Goman, 2011). While this may not seem fair, this is the way that the human brain is hardwired. It is very important that you are aware of how you are being perceived.

You are being viewed through the personal lens of your onlookers. They are formulating assumptions about you as an individual, along with the organization and/or profession you represent, based on their beliefs and value system. Onlookers are continually watching your behavior and listening to your language. They are listening to the words you choose and the tone in which you speak. When conversing with others, know how to adjust your elevator pitch for the individual or group you are speaking with. An elevator pitch is a "short summary of your service, product, or company and how it adds value to customers" (Riegel, 2013, p. 2). This is your opportunity to be influential and exercise your personal power while engaging with your new or existing network. This is also your chance to share your knowledge and skills.

Your verbal presentation is important, but your non-verbal presentation is equally important. By being well-groomed and clothed in business casual or business attire, you will be perceived as someone who is polished and well put together. Your posture and mannerisms will convey confidence in who you are as a person, and who you represent. Good eye contact and a firm handshake will convey you are sincere. Look attentive and project a positive attitude with a warm and genuine smile. Be a good listener and do not monopolize the conversation. This will keep the individual or group of people engaged longer, which will provide the opportunity to get to know them better. This will be beneficial for establishing and building relationships.

Tips:

- Make sure you have business cards available for those you wish to share your contact information

- Prepare your elevator pitch
- When conversing with others, be mindful of your tone. Be quick to listen, slow to speak, and slow to react
- Crossing your arms across your chest may be perceived as being closed minded and disinterested
- Be aware of the mannerisms and social cues of the individual or groups of people you are speaking with
- Try not to keep looking around the room when you are speaking with someone. Excuse yourself from the conversation first
- Remember, developing relationships, not just contacts, is key to having access to opportunities
- Your new or existing relationships could potentially lead to new opportunities

Exercise:

Write and practice an elevator pitch for presenting yourself, placing emphasis on your tone. If you have an upcoming event, tailor your elevator pitch for the group with whom you will be networking.

Chapter 3: Creating a Professional Portfolio

In this fast-paced healthcare environment where nursing jobs have become more competitive, differentiating yourself has become necessary for success and sustainability. Coupled with that, healthcare organizations are now challenged to do more with less, and recruitment and retention of talent has become a major priority.

Creating a professional portfolio can be a differentiator and set you apart from other nurses. A professional portfolio provides a tangible compilation of your education, skills and achievements that can provide prospective employers with samples and evidence that support the information on your resume and showcase your career. A professional portfolio can be used as a tool and resource for recruitment, retention, and promotion. Moreover, being familiar with the content of your portfolio will also help you articulate your strengths, skills, talents and abilities for successful results.

The contents of your professional portfolio should contain, but are not limited to:
- A copy of your resume or CV
- A copy of your nursing license and registration
- Your business card(s)
- A biographical summary
- A list of your professional references
- Copies of your certifications
- A list of professional organizations (local, state, national, and international) where you are a current member
- Patient care plans or educational material that you developed. Remember to remove any identifying information that would violate the Health Insurance Portability and Accountability Act (HIPAA)
- Any letters, thank you notes, awards, and/or recognitions that you have received that reflect your commitment to professional service excellence
- Copies of academic and continuing education courses, as well as conferences, seminars, workshops, and lectures you attend

- Any research or evidence based practice (Quality Assurance-Performance Improvement) activities that you are currently involved in or have participated in, at any level
- A list of all presentations and lectures you have given on a local, state, national, or international level
- Other information that reflects or highlights your professional practice or professional development such as when you are in the news, serve on community committees or volunteer

Tips:

- There is no right or wrong way or perfect time to create a professional portfolio
- Use a professional looking binder to keep all your documents. A plain white, dark blue or black binder is recommended. If you create a cover page for the binder, make sure that it too is professional looking. Avoid animals and flowers and other symbols that don't exemplify the nursing profession
- If you are a new nurse starting your career, now is a good time to begin the process
- If you are a more experienced nurse, the process will take you a bit longer to prepare your portfolio so strategically plan your steps. Your career did not develop overnight, and neither will your portfolio
- Commit to reviewing and revising your professional portfolio yearly. Performance appraisal time is a good way to remember it is time to update
- Bring your portfolio with you to all interviews

Exercise:

If you do not have a professional portfolio, begin the process of creating one today by collecting and organizing your supporting documents. If you have a professional portfolio, review it and update it as needed.

Chapter 4: Evaluating the Job Market

The new millennium has brought about changes in the way we conduct business in a global marketplace, including how we deliver healthcare. These changes pose new challenges for nurses to recognize opportunities to explore and create a strategic vision for growth and sustainability.

The economic downturn that occurred in 2008 was significant with lasting effects. Many Americans did not believe that it would be this bad for this long. While the "health care industry added 428,000 jobs throughout the 18-month recession from December 2007 until June 2009 and has continued to grow at a steady rate" (Wood, 2011, p. 13), nurses are finding it more challenging to enter the workforce following graduation from nursing school (CNNMoney, 2013). Other reasons that have contributed to a "tough market" are nurses are not retiring at the same rate as in previous years, along with the national movement for nurses to be minimally educated at the baccalaureate level.

In evaluating the job market, it is important to be aware of what is happening on a local, state and national level. The basic principles of supply and demand are alive and well. For example, if your perfect job includes working as a nurse in the specialty area of Labor and Delivery or Pediatrics, you may be living in a region where the market is already saturated with experienced nurses. As a new graduate, your chances of being considered for a position in these areas are almost non-existent. If you are determined to obtain a position in these areas, you may need to consider relocating to other areas, even out of state, where there is ample opportunity.

For experienced nurses exploring new opportunities it would be beneficial to revisit and revise your "perfect job" as described in the chapter, Getting Started. A more thorough examination will help you decide which options are available to you by narrowing necessary criteria. By writing and reviewing your perfect job description you will have a clearer understanding of what can be negotiated and what cannot.

For nurses at the executive level, the first question you should ask is "Am I willing to relocate?" If the answer is yes, this will increase your chances of achieving your career goals at a greater rate than if you are not willing to relocate. It will also open up many more doors of opportunities, professionally, personally, and often financially.

Tips:

- Do your research and know what fair market value is for the selected functional job description, as well as in the geographic area where you desire to practice
- Two reputable sites for salary comparison are:
  - Indeed.com
  - Salary.com
- Attend job fairs in the area where you desire to work
- Read job postings in nursing journals, as well as postings on the websites of professional nursing organizations and healthcare organizations/health system
- Reach out and network with persons currently working in the area(s) in which you are interested, via venues like professional nursing organizations, LinkedIn, or through colleagues and peers that can connect you to persons in the area

Exercise:

- Attend a workshop or seminar to prepare yourself to become market ready
- Explore *Fair Market Value* for specific positions and geographic areas of interest
- Explore geographic needs through professional websites such as *Salary.com* and *Indeed.com*
- Research the area through a variety of media such as the internet, social networking sites, and LinkedIn
- Attend Job Fairs
- Examine *Trend Reports* found in professional journals or online journals.

Chapter 5: Executive Summary

An Executive Summary is also known as the Professional Summary, Professional Qualifications, or Professional Profile. It is a brief summary or list that highlights your qualifications and gives the reader a "quick" glance at your professional qualifications and accomplishments, and what differentiates you. This section of information is used in place of the previously used resume objective. The information contained in this section highlights who you are (professionally), what you have achieved and how and what you can contribute. A well written Executive Summary prompts a closer read of your resume. When crafting an Executive Summary (Professional Summary, Professional Qualifications, or Professional Profile), be sure to quantify your statements with evidence. Using evidence supports your statement and strengthens it, taking it from an opinion to a fact.

Tips:

- Decide which heading to use Executive Summary, Professional Summary, Professional Qualifications, or Professional Profile, based upon where you are submitting your resume
- This section is a reference to your qualifications and accomplishments, but most importantly, it allows the reader of your resume to quickly identify what differentiates you from others
- Always quantify your statements and support with evidence. The evidence may need to be revised depending on where you are submitting your resume, and for what role
- Review this section and revise as needed, each and every time you submit your resume

Exercise:

Create an Executive Summary, Professional Summary, Professional Qualifications, or Professional Profile.

Figure 1. Sample Executive Summary

EXECUTIVE SUMMARY:
- Motivated achiever with strong leadership and problem solving skills; served as Nurse Manager and mentor for past seven years
- Effective written and verbal communicator with proven ability to understand and convey complex information; currently serve as a contributing member on several professional committees
- Award winning, excellent team builder with exceptional listening skills; received the Outstanding Nurse Manager Award in 2013
- Master's prepared Nurse Administrator
- Experienced Registered Nurse with nine years of clinical experience at a Level I Trauma Center

Figure 2. Sample Professional Profile

PROFESSIONAL PROFILE:
- Fast and willing learner who can grasp new ideas and operationalize them; current GPA 3.9
- Energetic, member of the healthcare team who can successfully manage priorities in a fast-paced environment; served as a Patient Care Technician in a busy surgical unit at an academic Medical Center
- Excellent team player who thrives in a collaborative environment comprised of diversely talented team members; extensive volunteer work
- Customer focused professional with expertise in building strong relationships necessary for innovation and growth; served as the Chair of the Service Recovery Committee for the past four years

Chapter 6: Biographical Summary

A biographical summary is a short story, between 150 to 350 words about you, and is a reflection of your professional credibility. A biographical summary is ever-evolving, and periodic changes need to be made to reflect the pertinent information that supports your credibility. A biographical summary is a useful tool for a variety of settings, which include, but are not limited to: being a presenter at a local, regional, national, or international event; your website; a press release; for consideration when joining a professional organization; networking; and for publication (about the author).

A biographical summary is an overview of your education, work experience and achievements that reflects your credibility and expertise. It is written in the third person. A biographical summary may or may not contain personal information and/or a photograph, this is optional. If a photograph is used it should be current. As you continue throughout your career journey you may have several versions of a biography at one time, each tailored to a specific focus of expertise.

Tips:

- Customize your biography for each specific focus of expertise. You want to be clear, concise, and accurate in portraying your information that supports your credibility
- Adhere to the 150 to 350 word limit, or what ever limit is specified
- This is an effective way for self-promotion without grandstanding
- Save every version of your biography because you may need to cut and paste when creating a new version

Exercise:

Create a biographical self profile. If you already have a biography, update it to reflect current education, experience and achievements.

Figure 1: Sample Biographical Summary

Add Photo Here (Optional)

Dr. Pamela C. Smith has more than thirty-five years of professional experience in healthcare and education. She has held a variety of entrepreneurial and innovative positions in leadership, management, practice and academics; serving as a provider, an educator, a leader, a mentor and a consultant.

Over the course of Dr. Smith's career, she had the opportunity to develop and implement new programs to meet current healthcare and educational needs. She has served in nursing leadership roles in both the inpatient and outpatient settings. She has worked as a staff nurse, a nurse manager, an operating room nurse, a clinical research nurse, a nurse practitioner, and a nurse educator. She was a founding member and the Director of the Center for Lifelong Learning, at the University of Rochester School of Nursing from 2001-2011. Dr. Smith's doctoral research examined professional development socialization and the process of role transition to identify the personal self for Registered Nurse First Assistants. In addition, Dr. Smith has served as a Legal Nurse Consultant and an independent leadership consultant for Ethicon Endo-Surgery, Inc, a Johnson & Johnson Company, Priority Thinking®, and The Academy for Leadership in Long-Term Care. Dr. Smith is currently a co-owner and co-founder of Class Act Consulting and Professional Development, and an Adjunct Instructor at the University of South Florida, College of Nursing and the University of Rochester, School of Nursing.

Over the course of her career, Dr. Smith has developed and delivered multiple presentations on a local, regional, and national level. She has taught courses at the baccalaureate, masters and doctoral levels of education. In addition, she has developed and delivered educational offerings for continuing professional education. She has also coached and mentored many individuals and groups, for successful results.

Figure 2: Sample Biographical Summary

Mary T. Birch, MS, RN is an expert in ambulatory care nursing. She is the Assistant Director of Ambulatory Services at the Western New York Office of Ambulatory Surgical Services. Mary brings a comprehensive history of experience and a wealth of knowledge to the position, which enables her to better lead and serve her patients, her staff and the organization with expertise and skill.

Mary has been a registered nurse for 10 years, and has worked in community-health, long term care, acute care and medical office settings as a staff nurse, a charge nurse, a nurse preceptor, a nurse educator, and currently as an Assistant Director. In 2004, she graduated from Baytown University College of Nursing with a master's degree. She is nationally certified in Ambulatory Care Nursing through the American Nurses Credentialing Center (ANCC), the world's largest and most prestigious nurse credentialing organization.

Chapter 7: Crafting a Professional Resume/Curriculum Vitae

A resume/curriculum vitae (CV) is a self-promotional tool that outlines your professional profile, your education, your pertinent professional experience, and your accomplishments. It may also contain other information such as community service and volunteer work. There is no one specific way to write a resume. It is most important that the information is well organized in an easy to read format. A well done resume/CV provides the end reader with a document that outlines your experience, strengths, skills, and abilities at a glance, and sets forth what differentiates you from other contenders.

A resume/CV is no longer exclusive to obtaining employment. Resumes are necessary for other venues, such as serving on a committee or board, presenting a professional presentation, submitting a manuscript for publication, or applying to an academic institution. A resume/CV is always a work in progress, and never a finished product. Resumes and CVs differ in length, type of information and focus. A resume is usually a maximum of two pages and must always be tailored to the specific position. A CV is predominately a lengthy document with a focus on academia.

When writing your resume, always ask yourself what differentiates me and what best promotes me? A resume should be tailored each time prior to sending it out. There are two types of resumes, namely; functional or chronological.

A **functional resume** is used by individuals with minimal experience and/or experience unrelated to their chosen career field. It is also used when there are gaps in work history. The purpose of the functional resume is to show transferable skills that have been acquired. These types of skills can include, but are not limited to the following:
- Management/Leadership Skills
- Communication
- Data and/or Financial Skills
- Organizational Skills
- Research Skills
- Teaching Skills
- Technical Skills

A **chronological resume** is most often used by individuals whose professional experience has predominately been in the same field, with little or no gaps in employment history. This format is reader friendly and requires a reverse chronology where you list your most recent professional experience first. A well done resume contains the following sections:

- Name
  Address • Telephone number • e-mail • LinkedIn address
- Professional Profile/Professional Summary/Qualifications (the points made in this section must be quantified-See Executive Summary chapter for more information)
- Education:
- Professional Experience:
- Professional Licenses/Accreditations/Memberships:
- Accomplishments/Achievements/Awards:
- Community Service:

References Available Upon Request is no longer necessary to add to your resume. Rather, references belong on a separate page (See Chapter 8 for more information on how to create a Reference page).

A CV differs from a resume in that it is more academically focused and is used when seeking positions related to academics, education, and scientific or research positions. The components of a CV are similar to a resume but contain other pertinent information. Another differentiator is that a CV contains multiple pages and is not limited. The components of a CV include:

- Name
- Address • Telephone • e-mail
- Education: (most recent first)
- Continuing Professional Education:
- Related Professional Experience: (Most recent first)
- Research/Grants/Teaching Experience:
- Fellowships:
- Professional Licenses/Accreditations/Memberships:
- Honors, Awards, and Service:
- Publications and Presentations:
- Manuscripts and Abstracts:
- Presentations and Academic Courses:

- Community Service:

As you proceed throughout your career, you may find that your resume begins to look more like a hybrid of both a resume and a CV. This is very common, and a differentiator for the nursing profession from other professions.

Exercise:

Create a resume or CV. If you already have a CV create a resume or vice versa. If you already have a resume/CV, update them now.

20

Figure 1: Sample Resume

Bella A. Perez

82 Sandstorm Drive, Anytown, NY 10555 ● (585) 555-5555 ● bella_perez@gmail.com

PROFESSIONAL PROFILE

- Motivated achiever with strong leadership and problem solving skills, served as unit preceptor and mentor for past seven years
- Effective written and verbal communicator with proven ability to understand and convey complex information, currently hold the position as the unit educator
- Award winning, excellent team builder with exceptional listening skills; current member of the Unit Council
- Master's prepared Adult Nurse Practitioner
- Experienced Registered Nurse with nine years of critical care experience at a Level I Trauma Center

EDUCATION
Masters of Science, Adult Nurse Practitioner   2013
York University, Belltone, NY

Relevant Nurse Practitioner Clinical Training
Exceptional Dermatology and Aesthetics Center, Mapleleaf, NY   Spring 2011
- Treated patients with acne, psoriasis, actinic keratosis, basal and squamous cell carcinomas
- Assisted in punch and shave biopsies, kenalog injections, procedures involving use of liquid nitrogen and electrocautery

Baskin Medical Center, Salmon Run, NY   Fall 2009/Spring 2010
- Diagnosed and treated adult patients with primary health care needs such as hypertension, hyperlipidemia, diabetes mellitus, emphysema and asthma
- Obtained comprehensive histories and performed physical assessments

Bachelor of Science in Nursing   1999
State University of York at Anytown, Anytown, NY

PROFESSIONAL EXPERIENCE
Registered Nurse   2007-present
Central Regional Medical Center-Trauma ICU, Mapleleaf, NY
- Provide comprehensive nursing care for patients with acute and traumatic conditions such as severe burns and skin grafts
- Unit educator for staff, patients and families
- Experience in wound debridement, ostomy, stoma, and decubitus ulcer care
- Experience with penetrating injuries, stabbings and gun shot wounds
- Provide care for patients with open and closed head injuries, brain aneurysms, spinal fractures, strokes, multi-system trauma, ventriculostomies, continuous dialysis and hemodynamic monitoring
- Knowledgeable in the mechanisms of action and titration of various continuously infusing sedatives, analgesics and vasopressors
- Advocate for patient and family needs

21

Flight Registered Nurse   2006-2009
Mercy Flight Central, Pleasantville, NY
- Provided care for critically ill patients of all ages needing rapid air transport by helicopter to tertiary care center
- Performed intubation, arterial and central line placement, intravenous and intraoseous line insertions, pericardial and thoracic needle decompression and surgical airways.

Registered Nurse, CVICU   2004-2007
Central Regional Medical Center, Mapleleaf, NY
- Provided comprehensive nursing care for patients following open-heart surgery, heart transplantation, intra-aortic balloon placement and heart failure patients requiring ventricular assist devices
- Proficient in continuous cardiac monitoring, arterial, central venous pressure monitoring and Swan-Ganz catheter monitoring.

Registered Nurse, Flex Team   1999-2003
Central Regional Medical Center, Mapleleaf, NY
- Provided nursing care for patients in different critical care settings
- Rotated among different intensive care units for six-week intervals
- Experienced is surgical, medical, cardiovascular and burn-trauma intensive care

LICENSES and CERTIFICATIONS
- Advanced Cardiac Life Support   2014-2016
- Basic Life Support   2014-2016
- Licensed Professional Registered Nurse State of New York #123456-1   1999

HONORS and AWARDS
- Star Award for Team Building - CR Medical Center-Trauma ICU   2009
- Preceptor of the Year Award - CR Medical Center-Trauma ICU   2009
- Featured Panelist - King Rounds regarding ethical issues - CR Medical Center   2008
- National Teaching Institute Award for Critical Care Nurses - CR Medical Center   2008
- Cardiac Intensive Care Unit (ICU) Nursing Award - CR Medical Center   2005

SKILLS
- Data Management: compiling information, calculations, managing records
- Technical: Proficient in the internet, Microsoft Office 2013 and several Electronic Medical Records (EMR) systems

Figure 2: Sample Curriculum Vitae (CV)

Pamela C. Smith
address ◆ e-mail ◆ phone number ◆ LinkedIn

Education:

University of Rochester Rochester, NY	Ed.D. Leadership in Higher Education	2011
University of Rochester Rochester, NY	Advanced Application for Legal Nurse Consulting	2002
University of Rochester Rochester, NY	Nurse Practitioner/Adult Primary Care	1997
University of Rochester Rochester, NY	M.S. (Nursing)	1997
University of Rochester Rochester, NY	B.S. (Nursing)	1994
Genesee Community College Batavia, NY	A.A.S. (Nursing)	1978

Conferences/Seminars/Workshops/Lectures Attended (Most Recent):

"Mainstreaming" Interprofessional Practice and Education (IPE)	Spring 2014
Finger Lakes Region Future of Nursing Conference	Spring 2013
Medical-Legal & Ethical Issues in Nursing	Spring 2013
Progress on the Institute of Medicine (IOM) Recommendations and Workforce Issues for New York State	Spring 2012

Professional Experience (Most Recent):

St. John Fisher College Wegmans School of Nursing, Rochester, NY	Adjunct Faculty	2013-2014
University of South Florida (USF) College of Nursing, Tampa, FL	Adjunct Instructor	2012-present
Class Act Consulting (co-Owner) & Professional Development Rochester, NY	Professional Coach, Healthcare Consultant & Leadership Educator	2008-present
Bausch & Lomb Rochester, NY	Legal Nurse Consulting	2008
Ethicon Endo-Surgery Division of Johnson & Johnson Cincinnati, Ohio	Leadership Consultant	2006-2007
University of Rochester School of Nursing	Adjunct Assistant Professor Assistant Professor of Clinical Nursing	2011-present 2011

23

Center for Nursing Entrepreneurship	Senior Associate of Clinical Nursing	2005-2011
Rochester, NY	Assistant Professor of Clinical Nursing	2004-2005
	Clinical Associate	2001-2004
	Director, Center for Lifelong Learning	2001-201

Honors, Awards and Service (Most Recent):

Association for Nursing Professional Development (member)	2014-present
American Organization of Nurse Executives Linked In (member)	2013-present
Future of Nursing-NYS Action Coalition: (member-Recommendation 2 & 6)	2013-present
PNEG | Professional Nurse Educators Group Linked In (member)	2012-present
Sigma Theta Tau (STT) International on LinkedIn (member)	2012-present
Sigma Theta Tau/Genesee Valley Nurses Association Research & Leadership Planning Committee (co-chairman)	2012-present
Sigma Theta Tau/GVNA Research and Leadership Planning Committee (member)	2009-present
Interviewed for article in NY Nurses Network, summer issue, and D & C (July 22)2009	
Senior Administrative Leadership Team (SALT) Committee (member)	2009-2011
Interviewed for article in NY Nurses Network, summer issue, and D & C (Aug. 14)	2008
Excellence Award in Career Counseling and Development	2006
Outstanding Faculty Colleague Award, University of Rochester School of Nursing 2004	
University of Rochester Center for Entrepreneurship (member)	2004-2011
Association of peri-Operative Registered Nurses (AORN member)	2002-2014
Sigma Theta Tau Intl. Honor Society of Nursing; Epsilon XI (inducted)	1995-present
Magna Cum Laude, University of Rochester	1994

Publications (Most Recent):
Manuscripts and Abstracts

Smith, P. C. (2011). A Study examining professional development socialization and the process of role transition to identify the personal self for students who have successfully completed the Registered Nurse First Assistant Program at the University of Rochester School of Nursing from 2005-2009. (Doctoral dissertation). Retrieved from UR Research at the University of Rochester. (11:36:19.127)

Smith, P. & VonBacho, S. (2007). An intrapreneurial initiative with an international reach: Online continuing education for nurses. Nurse Faculty Nurse Executive Summit, Nursing Economics. Scottsdale, AZ.

Academic Courses/Presentations (Most Recent):
Academic Courses

Spring 2014
"Organizational & Professional Dimensions of Nursing Practice" (NGR 6733)
University of South Florida College of Nursing, Tampa FL

"Web-Based Education for Staff Development" (NSP 3147)
University of South Florida College of Nursing, Tampa FL

"Foundations of Nursing Leadership" (GNUR 705-Doctorate of Nursing Practice)
Wegmans School of Nursing, St. John Fisher College, Rochester NY

"Nursing Leadership and Patient Centered Care III" (NURS 446)
Wegmans School of Nursing, St. John Fisher College, Rochester NY

Fall 2013
"Health Promotion Theories and Strategies Across the Lifespan" (NGR 6683)
University of South Florida College of Nursing, Tampa FL

"Skills for the Nursing Professional Development Educator" (NSP 4855)
University of South Florida College of Nursing, Tampa FL

"Evidence-Based Practice for the Baccalaureate Prepared Nurse" (NUR 4169C)
University of South Florida College of Nursing, Tampa FL

"Nursing Leadership and Patient Centered Care III" (NURS 446)
Wegmans School of Nursing, St. John Fisher College, Rochester NY

Summer 2013
"Nursing Research and Evidence-Based Practice" (NGR 6803)
University of South Florida College of Nursing, Tampa FL

"Systems and Populations in Healthcare" (NGR 6893)
University of South Florida College of Nursing, Tampa FL

"Evidence-Based Practice for the Baccalaureate Prepared Nurse" (NUR 4169C)
University of South Florida College of Nursing, Tampa FL

Spring 2013
"Nursing Leadership and Patient Centered Care III" (NURS 446)
Wegmans School of Nursing
St. John Fisher College, Rochester NY

"Health Promotion Theories and Strategies Across the Lifespan" (NGR 6683)
University of South Florida College of Nursing, Tampa FL

Presentations

2014
(September 25, 2014)
PPACA: What does this mean for you? Belmont-Central and Portage Park Chamber of Commerce
Meeting at Presence Health-Our Lady of the Resurrection Medical Center, Chicago, IL

(June 4, 2014)
"Employee Engagement & Team Building", Academy for Leadership in Long Term Care
St. John Fisher College Wegmans School of Nursing, Rochester NY

(June 3, 2014)
"Professional Development Socialization and the Process of Role Transition to Identify the
Personal Self for RN First Assistants", Registered Nurse First Assistant Program
University of Rochester School of Nursing, Rochester, NY

(February 4, 2014)
"Tapping into Your Entrepreneurial Spirit and Marketing Yourself", Role Seminar Nurse Practitioner Students, University of Rochester School of Nursing, Rochester, NY

2013
(October 5, 2014)
"Developing Professionally: Entrepreneurship in Nursing Practice"
Northeast Region Wound Ostomy and Continence Nurses Society and the Dermatology Nurses Association Conference, Rochester, NY

(March 4, 2013)
"Professional Development Socialization and the Process of Role Transition to Identify the Personal Self for RN First Assistants", Registered Nurse First Assistant Program
University of Rochester School of Nursing, Rochester, NY

(February 19, 2013)
"Tapping into Your Entrepreneurial Spirit and Marketing Yourself", Role Seminar Nurse Practitioner Students, University of Rochester School of Nursing, Rochester, NY

2012
(October 2, 2012)
"Organizational, Political and Personal Power"
Management of Care (NUR 371)
University of Rochester School of Nursing, Rochester, NY

(October 1, 2012)
"Professional Development Socialization and the Process of Role Transition to Identify the Personal Self for RN First Assistants", Registered Nurse First Assistant Program
University of Rochester School of Nursing, Rochester, NY

(September 5, 2012)
"Creating a Professional Development Toolkit"
 Senior Nursing Student Seminar, Nazareth College, Rochester, NY

(June 12, 2012)
"Organizational, Political and Personal Power"
Management of Care (NUR 371)
University of Rochester School of Nursing, Rochester, NY

Chapter 8: Professional References

Whether applying for a paid or unpaid position, the application process will most likely require a list of references. The gold standard is a minimum of three references, although you may be required to provide more. When considering who you would ask to serve as a reference, think about the position and the title of your references. This will add to the credibility of the reference. References should be people who can speak to your abilities and address their perception of how you would meet the qualifications of the specific job position or role.

When sending out a resume, a Reference page should be included as a separate document that contains a minimum of three references that are both credible and serve in a leadership capacity. This may include a supervisor at a recent place of employment, a faculty member, a department head, etc. Your references or types of references will depend upon the position in which you are applying. The necessary information should include:
- Name and credentials
- Title
- Company name, Address
- Telephone number, Fax number; E-mail address

Ask each reference, every time you use them, for permission before listing them. Give them a copy of your current resume and a copy of the job posting or functional job description. Discuss with your reference the type of recommendation they will give you. Ask your reference if there is a policy at the organization regarding references. Over the past years, organizations have established policies due to laws pertaining to defamation of character. Approximately one-half of all references get checked (Dourlain, 2011)

Tips:
- Prior to listing a person as a reference you must personally ask permission from them. This should be done each and every time you utilize them as a reference
- If someone agrees to be a reference indefinitely, you should notify them immediately when you use them as a reference.

This allows them the opportunity to be prepared if they are contacted
- Update your reference list regularly
- Ask your potential references if there is a policy at the organization where they work regarding what information can be disclosed
- Make sure that the reference is comfortable in serving as a beneficial reference
- The information included for each reference is the name of the reference and their credentials, their title, and their contact information such as phone number(s), email address, and business address. Make sure you only include the contact information approved by your reference
- The reference page is separate from your resume
- When attending an interview bring at least three copies of your reference list

Exercise:

Create a reference list with a minimum of three current references.

Figure 1. Example Reference Page

Susan T. Freeport, PhD, RN, APRN-BC, FAAN
Associate Dean of Nursing Graduate Studies
St. Binder College of Nursing
888 Miracle Drive
Northtown, NY 15555
(555) 555-5555
stfreeport@stbindercollege.edu

Greg S. Plant, MS, RN, NEA-BC
Chief Nursing Officer
Central Regional Medical Center
343 10th Ave
New York, NY 10101
(555) 444-3333
gsplant@crmc.newyork.org

Keri B. Cutter, MS, RN
Nurse Manager, Trauma Intensive Care Unit
Central Regional Medical Center
343 10th Ave
New York, NY 10101
(555) 444-3322
kbcutter@crmc.newyork.org

Chapter 9: Cover Letter

A cover letter is essential whether you are applying for your first nursing position, for an executive leadership position, or any nursing position in between. The cover letter document is the first time a prospective employer or the reader "meets" you, the candidate. A cover letter allows the reader to focus on your credentials and the specific aspects of your background that qualify you for the position. Writing a cover letter allows you to explain why you are interested in the position and the organization. A cover letter should enhance, and not duplicate the contents of your resume/CV, and prospective employers and hiring managers often read the cover letter first. A well written cover letter encourages a thorough reading of your resume/CV.

We currently live in the era of electronic applications and although a cover letter is not always required, it is highly recommended. For some employers, a cover letter is a reflection of the candidate's commitment to the position. It also shows the employer that you are able to articulate your strengths, skills, talents, and abilities and emphasize why this position is a "best fit" for you.

When writing a cover letter, the essential components of a cover letter include:
- Introduction, why are you writing
- What your experience/education offers
- Why are you interested in the position and the organization
- What will happen next i.e. Thanking the prospective employer for considering your application and expressing your desire to advance to the next level with an actual interview

Make sure that there are no typographical errors or mistakes. Proof reading your cover letter with a critical eye and correcting errors and mistakes prior to submission can prevent you from being interpreted as careless and sloppy.

Tips:
- Keep a cover letter to one page in length

- Ask others to proof read your cover letter to make sure there are no mistakes. A fresh pair of eyes offers a new prospective and often times the reader can pick up mistakes that you missed
- Customize your cover letter every time you submit one
- You may need to combine your cover letter and your resume into one document in order to submit them electronically
- Makes sure that the formatting is correct and the fonts are the same

Exercise:

Select a job description that interests you and write a cover letter addressing the components listed above. Conclude the cover letter with a paragraph thanking the hiring manager or prospective employer for their consideration, emphasizing that you would greatly appreciate the opportunity to interview. Make sure to include your contact information.

Figure 1: Sample Cover Letter

January 28, 2014

(Put 5 spaces between the date and the name of the person to whom you are writing)

Mary Beth Taylor, MS, RN
Nurse Recruiter
Wellness Health System
42 Large Circle
New Town, NY 14625
(555) 999-2222

(Put 3 spaces between the address and the salutation)

Dear Ms. Taylor,

I recently learned about your position for an Intensive Care Registered Nurse, reference number 54746, from the Wellness Health System website. After reviewing the job description and the qualifications, I believe there would be a good fit between my skills and interests and this position. I have attached a copy of my resume for your review.

I became familiar with the healthcare environment early in life because both my parents were employed in the healthcare industry as Registered Nurses. I spent time with them at their places of employment. It was in 2009 when I began to consider a career in nursing. During the summer of 2009, a very close friend of mine was diagnosed with a terminal illness and I found myself wanting to be a part of her care. I found myself assuming the advocacy role for my friend, which gave me the opportunity to experience the healthcare system from the patient's perspective. Her disease process was aggressive and she passed several months later. Shortly after that experience, another close friend was involved in a motor vehicle accident. She spent several days in an ICU and I was there each day by her side. It was during that time that I had the opportunity to observe the nursing staff and the way they interacted with patients, their families, and other members of the health care team. I was also impressed with their knowledge and skills. These two experiences had a direct impact on my desire to pursue a career in nursing, and hopefully secure a position in an ICU.

I have a strong work ethic and I am capable of working in a fast paced environment as evidenced by my successful completion of an accelerated baccalaureate nursing program. I believe my greatest strengths are my communication skills and my ability to be an excellent team player and a good colleague. This is evidenced in my resume during my previous work experience as a Patient Care Technician for the Wellness Healthcare System, and the Customer Service Representative for the Home Improvement Store. I am self-directed, organized, and my values align with the values of the Wellness Health System which focuses on patient and family centered care. I would be honored to be selected to join your nursing team.

Thank you for your consideration of my application. I look forward to hearing from you to set up an interview at a mutually convenient time. I can be reached by phone at (585) 555-2222, or via e-mail at njones33@gmail.com

(Put 3 spaces between the last paragraph and your closing remark)
Sincerely,

Nancy M. Jones

Nancy M. Jones
3218 North Road
Mytown, NY 12345

Figure 2. Sample Cover Letter

November 14, 2014

(Put 5 spaces between the date and the name of the person to whom you are writing)

Mr. William Chips
Chief Human Resource Officer
Westside Health System
Administration Building-Box 123
102 South Street
Anywhere, NY 15555

(Put 3 spaces between the address and the salutation)

Dear Mr. Chips,

I recently learned of your need for an Adult Nurse Practitioner with the orthopaedic practice at Westside Health System. After reviewing the requirements of the position, I believe there would be a good fit between my skills and interests and this position. Currently, I am employed as an orthopedic nurse at the Seaside Trauma Center in Hometown, NY. In addition, I am a Nurse Practitioner student, and I will complete my Adult Nurse Practitioner Program at Excellent University, College of Nursing in May 2015.

As evidenced by my resume, I have over 12 years of nursing experience serving as both a provider and a leader working in a variety of settings, with diverse populations. I had the benefit of caring for individuals with orthopaedic needs, providing primary prevention education, to caring for those who are acutely ill. Over the course of my career, I have sought out positions where I can utilize my knowledge and skills to increase the health, wellness, and well-being of patients and their families. I was recently part of the team that developed new patient education materials at Seaside Trauma Center. I attribute my continued success to my commitment to ongoing professional and personal development, as well as working as a collaborative team member. I believe my greatest strengths include being a motivated, self-directed individual with detailed organizational skills. I am also a strong communicator focused on building and sustaining relationships.

I would be honored to be selected to be part of the orthopaedic healthcare team at Westside Health System that is dedicated and committed to service and operational excellence, as well as improving and maintaining the health of the citizens within the communities they serve. I am confident I possess the knowledge and skills necessary to be a valuable asset to your organization.

Thank you for your consideration of my application and resume. I look forward to hearing from you to set up an interview at a mutually convenient time. I can be reached by e-mail at Susan_Sunshine@gmail.com or by phone at 585-555-5555.

Sincerely,

Susan R. Sunshine

Susan R. Sunshine, MS, RN
4378 Brick Road
Somewhere, NY 15555

Chapter 10: Transcript Summaries

A transcript summary is a summarized version of your academic history, performance and course descriptions. Potential employers require verification that the applicant has met the criteria pertinent to the position applied for, and the applicant is in good standing. The transcript summary is required across the board from entry level positions to executive level positions. A formal transcript summary is requested by the applicant to be sent "officially" directly to the organization and does not go via the individual. This transcript is certified to ensure the integrity of the document.

When applying for an internship, a transcript summary may be necessary to aid the perspective employer in determining if the applicant is qualified for the position. The transcript summary verifies the course work to date has been successfully completed. Transcript summaries can be the differentiator in being hired. Many times, when multiple applicants are vying for one position, class standing, as well as the courses completed within the program curriculum, may be the deciding factor in the applicant being offered the internship opportunity.

An informal transcript summary contains the same information as an official transcript summary without the seal of authenticity. It is recommended that the individual retain a copy of the unofficial transcript summary for their records so that they are aware of what information is included in the document.

Tips:

- You should always have an unofficial copy of your transcript summary in your possession
- Keep an itemized list of all academic institutions you attended, with addresses including web addresses, and telephone numbers
- There are three ways to request a formal transcript summary
  - Telephone
  - Electronically
  - Postal Service

- Be aware that there may be a fee associated with a request for a formal transcript(s) summary. More than likely, you will have to pay a fee for each individual transcript ordered

Exercise:

Request an unofficial copy of your transcript(s) for your files. Know what information is contained in your transcript summary. This will help you better articulate the strengths and weaknesses of your academic history.

Chapter 11: Background & Credit Checks

Performing a background and/or credit check on nurses was virtually unheard of years ago. Now, in today's current healthcare environment, a background check has become commonplace to verify college degrees and professional licenses, previous employment, as well as uncover any legal or criminal issues (Advanced Research Systems [ARS], 2011). While less common, credit checks might be performed if the job requirement has a major financial component. A credit check will reveal information such as bankruptcies, foreclosures and late payments (ARS, 2011). Laws can vary on checking criminal history depending on the state.

According to the Joint Commission (2008), a criminal background check is now required for "staff, students and volunteers who work in the same capacity as staff who provide care, treatment, and services, as required by law, regulation and organization policy" (The Joint Commission, 2012, para. 1). This requirement was initiated following the Charles Cullen case and other incidents. Charles Cullen was a Registered Nurse (RN) who confessed to murdering 30-45 people over the course of 16 years, in hospitals in Pennsylvania and New Jersey, in spite of being fired at least five times from previous facilities (CBSNEWS.com, 2013).

Consent to perform a background check and/or credit check is often found embedded in the application process. This is generally located around the area where you will attest that the information you have provided is accurate and truthful. There may be an additional cost to you for the background check.

Tips:
- Always read the application or contract thoroughly, even the fine print
- Do not sign anything without first reading and understanding what you are signing
- Ask questions for clarification if you do not understand something

- By law, you are eligible to obtain a free copy of your credit report every 12 months
- "The Federal Trade Commission (FTC), the nation's consumer protection agency, enforces the Fair Credit Reporting Act (FCRA), a law that protects the privacy and accuracy of the information in your credit report" (Federal Trade Commission, 2013, para. 4). More information can be found on the website at http://www.consumer.ftc.gov/articles/0157-employment-background-checks
- "An employer must get your permission before asking for a report about you from a credit reporting company or any other company that provides background information" (Federal Trade Commission, 2013, para. 9)
- If you know what information will be discovered in your background or credit check, you can prepare to address the questions that may be asked
- If you have events in your life that may be considered questionable, or may be contained in your background check, you may want to consider seeking legal council from a lawyer who specializes in employment law, or contact the state Office of Professional Misconduct
- If you believe you were not offered a position due to the information contained in your background or credit check, the employer has a legal obligation to show you the report and tell you how to obtain a copy. More information can be found on The Federal Trade Commission website at http://www.consumer.ftc.gov/articles/0157-employment-background-checks

Exercise:

Before you apply for a job, order a free copy of your credit report. The three free credit report companies are: TransUnion, Equifax, and Experian.

Chapter 12: Social Networking

The use of technology and electronic communication has permeated healthcare and has become an integral part of our daily operations, both professionally and personally. The National Student Nurse's Association [NSNA] defines social media "as web-based and mobile platforms for user generated content that create interactive and highly accessible, and often public, dialogues" (n.d., para. 2). Moreover, the American Nurses Association [ANA] has adopted the definition of social networks proposed by Boyd and Ellison in 2007 "as web-based services that allow individuals to 1) construct a public or semi-public profile within a bounded system, 2) articulate a list of other users with whom they share a connection, and 3) view and traverse their lists of connections and those made by others within the system" (2011, para. 2).

Social media sites such as Facebook, LinkedIn, YouTube, Instagram, as well as the many others on a long list that can be found through a Google search, have made it easy to connect and stay connected with friends, family, and business constituents globally. This technology has brought to light both positive benefits and negative consequences. The positive benefits of social media include, but are not limited to, an increase in the ability to network, communicate and build relationships with people you do not see face-to-face on a regular basis; provide a forum to promote the respectful exchange of knowledge and resources, as well as research and best practices. Social media also provides a venue for "educating the public on nursing and health related matters" (ANA, 2011, para. 4). In addition, social media sites provide opportunities that would not normally be available by other means. An example would be searching for someone with a specific knowledge or expertise for a job posting, for research, for publication, or a presentation.

While the benefits of social media are many, there are negative consequences associated with the improper use. The posting of information can be a breach of confidentiality, a loss or invasion of privacy, which can result in professional and unethical misconduct and moral turpitude. These consequences can impede the public trust of the nursing profession, cause loss of employment and lead to legal liability. Many employers are practicing due diligence in reviewing social media sites for prospective and current employees.

Tips:

- Protect your nursing license by educating yourself in regards to what information is acceptable to share and what is not when using social media
- Add a link to the ANA Code of Ethics for Nurses, National Council of State Boards of Nursing Social Media Guidelines, and American Nurses Association (ANA) Social Networking Principles Toolkit to your favorites on your electronic devices, and refer to them regularly

Exercise:

- Visit the National Council of State Boards of Nursing website; Social Media Guidelines at https://www.ncsbn.org/2930.htm, and review the information and videos
- Visit the American Nurses Association (ANA) Social Networking Principles Toolkit at http://www.nursingworld.org/socialnetworkingtoolkit
- Review your social media accounts (Facebook, Twitter, LinkedIn, YouTube, etc.) for potential violations and revise the information contained in your account, as necessary
- Locate and review the social media policy at the organization(s) where you work

Chapter 13: Prepping for an Interview

You have just scheduled an interview and it is time to plan ahead. Before the day of your interview you will want to learn as much as possible about the organization in regards to the market place (region where the organization is located, types of goods and services offered, and the local economy), who are their customers and stakeholders, reputation of the organization, and competitors. Researching this information via the internet, speaking with current and past employees, and reading any written material about the organization will help you during the interview to answer potential questions and formulate questions of your own.

In planning for the interview, it is important to dress appropriately, selecting a well-groomed professional look. Dress conservatively and avoid bright, flashy colors and patterns, to convey confidence and self-assurance. Solid navy blue, medium to dark gray or brown colors are usually best (Doyle, 2014). While it is preferable to wear a suit, a color-coordinated blazer, pastel blouse, and long skirt or slacks can be worn. For men, it is recommended that you wear a button down shirt and a tie with your suit. Different colors can influence emotion and symbolize certain meanings. For example, the color blue is associated with the terms calm, trust, confidence and truth, to name a few (Incredible @ rt Department, n.d.). Whereas the color grey is associated with the terms security, reliability, intelligence, and maturity (Incredible @ rt Department, n.d.). The color brown is associated with the terms stability, reliability, comfort, and endurance (Incredible @ rt Department, n.d.). Wear comfortable clothing that is clean and pressed. This pertains to all clothing from a suit to scrubs. While it is recommended that you wear slacks, if you must wear a skirt make sure that your hosiery is skin colored. In addition, wear polished shoes. Wear low-heeled, conservative closed-toed dress shoes that are color coordinated with your outfit. This shows your impeccable attention to detail. If you need to wear a belt, wear a dress belt that matches your shoes.

Keep jewelry to a minimum and avoid jewelry that distractively jingles or swings when you move. Facial jewelry should be removed, although it is acceptable to wear small, conservative earrings, only one per ear in the traditional earlobe position. Cover your tattoos. Many healthcare organizations now have policies regarding piercings and tattoos. Apply makeup sparingly and avoid unusual or bright colors. While it is preferable to not wear any perfume or cologne, if you must wear it, use it sparingly. Style your hair tastefully (err on the conservative side) or have it professionally done (Doyle, 2014). While wearing clear or no nail polish is best, avoid fingernail designs and bright colored polish.

Empty your pockets of things that jingle to avoid the temptation to nervously play with them during the interview. In addition, it is better to carry a briefcase or portfolio into an interview, rather than a purse. Bringing a briefcase or a portfolio provides the medium to carry supporting documents and other documents with you. This keeps the number of articles you bring to the interview to a minimum.

On the day of the interview it is important to be punctual. If you will be traveling to an area that you are unfamiliar with, you may want to take a trial run a day or two before. Keep track of how long it takes you to drive to your destination. You may want to allow extra time, depending upon traffic patterns. Also, locate where you will be parking. If it is a pay parking lot you will want to make sure that you bring money to exit the parking lot. Confirm the time of your interview and arrive early, at least 10-15 minutes before the scheduled time. Do not arrive any earlier because it can cause confusion. Arriving too late creates a bad impression.

On the day of the interview make sure you are prepared. Bring all relevant information and verification documents such as: a copy of your tailored resume and cover letter, two forms of identification, a copy of your nursing license/registration, copies of your certification(s) and a list of your references. Bring at least three copies of each.

During the interview, watch your body language. Sit upright in your chair with both feet on the floor, poised slightly forward. Your non-verbal language is important, look attentive, do not slouch in your chair, and project a positive attitude with a warm and genuine smile. Good eye contact and a firm handshake will convey you are genuinely happy to be invited to the interview. Be prepared to answer open-ended behavioral based questions. It is common belief that previous behavior is a good predictor of future behavior because it requires a response based upon specific examples of past experiences.

During the interview, it is recommended that you do not initiate the conversation about salary. Let the interviewer or hiring manager address this question first. You may have a preconceived salary figure that you are considering; when in reality you have undervalued your contribution to the organization and the position. Knowing fair market value for the position prior to the interview will benefit you greatly.

Towards the end of the interview, the interviewer will ask you if you have any questions, and you should be prepared. Prior to the interview, create a list of 3-5 questions to ask. Your questions should reflect your professional attitude and motivation. If the questions you prepared were answered during the interview, ask another question or ask for clarification of something the interviewer said during the interview. Asking questions during an interview indicates you did your research prior to the interview and also conveys your interest in the organization. Not asking questions can be perceived as being uninterested or unprepared. Never lie or hedge in an interview. Always tell the truth. If you have questions about events in your life that may be perceived as questionable, you may want to seek legal council with an attorney who specializes in employment law prior to the interview. The interview is your time to explain situations or events that may appear questionable, such as termination from a previous employer, grades or courses on your transcript summary, gaps in your work history, etc.

At the close of the interview, ask when you might expect to hear back from someone in the organization regarding the position. You can also ask about the anticipated time frame for filling the position.

Tips:

- Avoid wearing all black or all red. The color black is often associated with the terms power, arrogance, wealth, death and fear, to name a few. The color red is often associated with the terms power, aggression, danger, fire, and strength (Incredible @ rt Department, n.d.)

- Don't wait until the last minute to plan your outfit to wear on an interview. This will help you avoid undue stress and pressure to buy costly clothing items you wouldn't normally buy
- You don't need to spend a lot of money on a suit or a jacket and dress pants. Shop around for sales and buy a classic suit that is always in style. Also, consider shopping at consignment shops or shops that sell gently used clothes
- In preparation for the interview, familiarize yourself with questions that your prospective employer may ask that are inappropriate and/or illegal. A good resource from the Office of Human Resources at the National Institute of Health can be found at http://hr.od.nih.gov/hrguidance/employment/interview/
- It is important to prepare for the behavioral interview questions regarding your performance, and professional conduct. Think about actual situations in your past or current work settings and practice telling your story. Your story can be a differentiator that sets you apart from other applicants
- You will most likely be asked a question about your strengths and weaknesses. Be prepared to answer these questions. When articulating your strengths use descriptive words and support with evidence. Your strengths should reflect the information you have on your resume and cover letter (see the Chapter 7 Crafting a Professional Resume/Curriculum Vitae, Chapter 9 Cover Letter, and Chapter 5 Executive Summary). When addressing your weaknesses, it is recommended that you discuss weaknesses that you can improve on. For example if the position you have applied for requires you to create Excel Spreadsheets and that is an area of weakness for you, you can report that you are taking a continuing professional education class on how to create Excel Spreadsheets. Make sure you are really registered for the class
- Turn your cell phone off prior to the interview. A ringing or buzzing cell phone is a major distraction and the hiring manager may consider this a deal breaker
- If you are asked a question that has two or three parts, make

sure you answer all parts. If you aren't sure if you answered all parts, ask the interviewer to repeat the question
- If the opportunity for a shadowing experience is not offered, you may want to considering asking for one
- Let the interviewer or hiring manager initiate the discussion regarding salary

Exercise:

Assess your wardrobe for appropriate attire to wear to an interview. Make sure that all articles of clothing fit properly and that your shoes are polished. Review the sample interview questions provided and formulate your answers to the questions. Practice telling your story so that during the interview your answers are relaxed and natural rather than scripted and rehearsed.

Figure 1. Sample Interview Questions You May Be Asked During an Interview (This is not an all inclusive list)

- What are your strengths?
- What qualifications do you have that make you think you will be successful in this position?
- What are your weaknesses and areas for growth?
- What are your two most satisfying professional accomplishments?
- How do you handle stress?
- Why would you like to work for us?
- What is most important to you in a job?
- What style of leadership/management do you work best under?
- Describe a situation when you prevented a problem before it occurred? What was the problem? What did you learn from the situation?
- Describe a time when you went above and beyond to provide customer service. What was the outcome?
- What do you know about our organization?
- Tell me about a time in which you had to handle an irate physician, co-worker, patient or family member? How did you handle it? What were the results?
- Describe a situation where there wasn't a trusting relationship between you and a co-worker or boss. What did you do to try to improve the relationship?
- Describe a difficult decision you've made, the process you went through to arrive at the decision, and the outcome?
- Why should I hire you?
- How long would you stay if we offered you this position?

Figure 2. Sample Questions To Ask In An Interview (This is not an all inclusive list)

- What are the current challenges that your organization faces?
- What would be my primary challenges if I were selected for this position?

- What are the primary functions I would be performing in this role?
- What is the organizational policy regarding financial and other support in continuing professional education?
- What is your assessment of my status for this position?
- When can we meet again?

Chapter 14: Post-Interview Thank You

You have just completed that long awaited interview and now it is time to properly thank your interviewer(s). Your interview may have been with one interviewer or several. Do not forget to ask for a business card from each of the individuals that interview you. If they do not have a business card, make sure that you obtain their name (the correct spelling) and their credentials at the time of the interview. This will help expedite the post-interview thank you process. A post-interview thank you note should be written as soon as possible after the interview, usually within the following one to two days. A post interview thank you note is a respectful way to thank the interviewer for their time, and also another opportunity for you to restate your interest in the position. A post-interview "thank you" can sometimes be a differentiator for you, setting you apart from other contenders for the position.

Tips:

- Ask for a business card from each of the individuals that interview you. A business card will contain the correct spelling of the person's name, their credentials, title and contact information
- Make sure that you have the correct spelling and title of the name of the person you are writing to
- Writing a hand written thank you note is more personal than sending an e-mail. A hand written thank you note is the preferred method, although it may not be the most efficient
- A blank thank you note is preferred and looks more professional than a pre-printed note
- If you forgot to obtain a business card at the interview, do not hesitate to obtain the necessary information via the organizations web site or by making a telephone call
- The internet provides multiple examples of what information to include in a post interview thank you note
- Writing a post interview thank you note provides a good reason to generate a follow up phone call

Craft a post-interview thank you note.

Figure 1: Post-Interview Thank You Note Example

October 27, 2014

Dear Ms. Jones,

It was a pleasure to meet with you in person on Monday, October 27th, 2015. I appreciate you taking the time to get to know me and to answer all my questions. I learned a lot from our conversation and I appreciate you sharing your experiences. Our interview, as well as the other interviews, has affirmed for me that working at Acme Medical Center would be a good fit with my skills and interests.

Thank you again for your generosity with your time. I look forward to hearing your decision about my candidacy for the Registered Nurse position in the Medical Intensive Care Unit (MICU).

Best regards,

Susan R. Sunshine, MS, RN-BC

Figure 2: Post-Interview Thank You Note Example

October 27, 2014

Dear Dr. Memory,

Thank you so much for taking the time out of your busy schedule to interview me on Monday, October 27, 2014. I enjoyed our conversation, and I appreciate your candor about the position and the challenges for the person in the role of the Chief Nursing Officer. I believe that the position will be a good fit with my education, experience, skills and interests; and I view the challenges we discussed as opportunities. I believe my many years of experience in healthcare serving in a variety of leadership and management positions, as well as my experience working with multiple accrediting agencies, has prepared me to be successful in this role. I believe I would be an asset to the Acme Health System team in moving the mission and vision forward.

Thank you again for your generosity with your time, and your consideration of me for this position. I look forward to hearing back from you regarding your decision.

Best regards,

Susan R. Sunshine, MS, MBA, RN-BC

Chapter 15: How to Evaluate a Job Offer

You have completed the interview process and have now received the long awaited job offer. When evaluating a job offer you will want to consider the four C's; Content, Culture, Compensation, and Challenge before negotiating the contract.

Content

When considering the actual job description and the job you will be performing, you should ask yourself the following questions. Is this role a good fit with my skills and interests? Will this position allow me to use the skills I enjoy, and what percentage of the time will be allocated to performing these skills? What will be my role in the organization in regards to leadership, autonomy, visibility, and decision making?

Culture

When considering culture, this refers to the culture of the organization (the underlying set of key values, beliefs, understandings, and norms shared by employees). Reflect back on the interview process, the people you interviewed with, and the guided tour of the organization. Pay attention to how you felt during the interview process. Did you feel excited yet relaxed, or anxious and concerned? What was the identified leadership or management style of your prospective supervisor, as well as the leadership or management style of the organization? Did the behaviors and actions of the people you came in contact with reflect the identified style? Were the employees happy and helpful? Was teamwork and collaboration clear and evident? What is the reputation of the organization held by the employees, by the members of the community? If the reputation of the organization is in question, what are the challenges that the organization is experiencing and what are the proposed strategies to address the challenges? What is the communication process within the organization, and is this process practiced by the employees? How does the organization support the professional and personal development of the staff?

Compensation

When considering compensation, realize this encompasses more than your hourly rate or annual salary. Compensation also includes benefits and perks. Your salary amount will be concrete, whereas your benefits and perks may vary and can be negotiable. By understanding what benefits and perks are available, you will be better prepared to evaluate the job offer. Benefits to consider may include; health and dental insurance; sick, personal, and vacation days, also known as paid time off (PTO); life insurance; retirement plans; stock options and profit sharing. Perks may include reimbursement for continuing professional development such as college tuition, seminars, and workshops; technology access such as a paid cell phone and/or computer; mileage reimbursement; and longevity benefits.

Challenge

When evaluating the challenge of the job that you have been offered, you will want to consider your professional development and autonomy in the position. Based upon your career direction, you may want to reflect on the challenges the organization is currently facing and the challenges you may face with respect to accepting the position. Ask yourself; Am I up for the challenge(s)? Are the events in my personal life conducive for taking on these challenges? Will I be supported, both professionally and personally, to achieve success and sustainability? Do I currently have the necessary tools and resources to seek the support I need?

Tips:

- Review the proposed job offer/package carefully and then set it aside for a day or two and then re-evaluate to provide a fresh perspective
- Try to avoid making an instantaneous decision to accept the position, rather respectfully ask for at least 24 hours, up to one week to review the job offer/package and discuss the pros and cons of accepting the position with key people in your life such as; significant other, spouse, parents, children, etc.
- Perform a written cost/benefit analysis, evaluating the pros and cons of accepting the job offer/package
- Determine what parts of the job offer/package are non-negotiable and negotiable

Re-read and thoroughly review the description of your perfect job that you completed in Chapter 1: Getting Started. Complete the elements of your perfect job in relationship to location, job duties, financials, hours per work week, and anything else that matters to you to see if they still apply for this job offer/package? If not, this would be the time to re-evaluate and re-write your perfect job description.

Chapter 16: Negotiating a Contract

In Chapter 15: How to Evaluate a Job Offer, you evaluated the recent job offer with regards to the four C's; Content, Culture, Compensation, and Challenge and are excited about reviewing the contract. As mentioned earlier in Chapter 13 Prepping for an Interview, you should not initiate the conversation about salary. Let the interviewer or hiring manager address this question first. You may have a preconceived salary figure that you are considering; when in reality you have undervalued your contribution to the organization and the position. If you bring up the salary amount first, the hiring manager may be more than happy to pay you what you asked for because it was considerably less than what they were willing to pay. The way to avoid this mistake is to know ahead of time what fair market value is for the position in this particular location. Fair market value can differ depending upon geographic location, where the laws of supply and demand rule.

Be prepared to negotiate and go for the win-win situation. First articulate what you liked about the original contract. Know what you are willing to negotiate and what you need to stand firm on. Never make demands, but rather raise questions. More importantly, make sure you have prepared questions. Clarify your goals and ask them to clarify theirs. Listen carefully to the expectations and interests being expressed by the hiring manager. Focus on the needs of the organization.

When submitting a counter proposal, use evidence from credible sources to support your claims. Include a few benefits that are expendable. Use positive language and negotiate to your strengths, whether it is written or verbal. If salary is non-negotiable, consider bargaining for other benefits and/or perks. Negotiate your base salary first before negotiating the other elements of the contract. Never stop selling yourself and keep a positive attitude. Remember, the negotiation process is not personal. Rather it is about finding a place that is acceptable to both parties to create a win-win situation.

Tips:

- Do your research and know what fair market value is for the

position and geographic location. Websites like Indeed.com and Salary.com will allow you to search by position and location
- Be clear on your goals and your expected outcome(s) before entering into negotiations
- Be prepared to negotiate and compromise and don't feel pressured to sign the contract immediately. It is acceptable to ask for a reasonable time, generally three to seven days, to review and consider the terms and conditions of the contract
- You may want to consider having your lawyer review the contract before you sign it
- Ask for clarification if you do not understand. Once you sign a contract you no longer have the ability to negotiate and are now legally bound by the terms and conditions
- Salary is important but other things you may want to consider include: work environment (culture fit), benefits, and perks
- It is okay to say thank you for the offer but no thank you to the position if you are not happy with the terms and conditions. Remember you have a choice and can exercise your choice

Exercise:

Search the internet for sample nursing contracts. Review the nursing contracts to familiarize yourself with the layout of the contract, the verbiage, and what is generally included. This will help you in the future when you are reviewing a contract to know what is standard and what needs to be added to the contract.

Chapter 17: Assessments

Talent assessments, also known as pre-employment screening tests are now currently being utilized in healthcare. These types of assessments and tests have been in place for many years in the business world. These tools are used to gain insight into cognitive ability, behavior, and dependability for the individual. "Talent assessments help predict a prospective applicant's on-the-job performance and retainability, so in theory, applicants that pass the screening test should perform better as employees if they're hired" (Doyle, 2014, para. 2). Many of the assessments/tests are performed electronically for instantaneous results, and may be administered prior to the actual interview. The results may or may not be shared with the prospective employee.

Pre-employment assessments and tests administered by the prospective employer should be both valid and reliable, which means they were created using research. Validity is defined as quality of being logically or factually sound (Merriam-Webster, 2014). A valid assessment/test will predict a prospective employee's performance in the area for which the assessment/test was intended (Mercer, 2014). Whereas, the reliability of the assessment/test procedure will yield the same results on repeated attempts (Merriam-Webster, 2014). The three most common types of assessments/tests are cognitive ability assessments/tests such as; problem-solving, vocabulary and word use ability; behavior assessments/tests such as personality traits and motivations; and dependability assessments/tests such as work ethic and trustworthiness. The results of these assessments/tests can also help predict whether or not the prospective applicant would be a "good fit" within the organizational culture. Categories of assessments\tests can include but are not limited to:
- Leadership/Management Style Assessments
- Organizational Behavior/Culture Assessments
- 360 Assessments
- Personality Assessments
- Strong Inventory Assessments

Tips:

58

- When asked to complete an assessment/test, answer the questions honestly giving your "best" answer. Some assessments/tests contain a distortion factor which pertains to not answering the questions consistently
- Ask what type(s) of pre-employment testing will be administered
- Some of the pre-employment assessments/tests are timed. It is important that you schedule a time when you will not be interrupted or rushed while taking the test
- While you may experience some test taking anxiety, it is important to take the required assessments/tests when you are feeling calm and focused

Exercise:

This exercise will expose you to the types of questions and formatting that may appear on other assessments/tests. It will also provide you with a personality profile and insight into your characteristics. Search the internet for a free personality test, such as the Keirsey Temperament Sorter®-II (KTS®-II), found at http://www.keirsey.com/sorter/register.aspx

Chapter 18: Coaching & Mentoring

The developmental technique of coaching, initially associated with sports, has become an accepted practice in the business community, and most recently in healthcare. The coaching technique is individualized and tailored to meet the specific developmental needs of the person being coached. This technique increases the chances of success and provides the best possible outcomes for both the individual and the organization. Coaching provides benefits that other change and growth strategies do not offer.

Coaching and the technique of mentoring have a place in the ever-changing healthcare environment where nurses face multiple day-to-day challenges. While the terms coaching and mentoring are often used interchangeably, they differ in context. Coaching is a more formal process that is goal-directed, action-oriented, and time-limited. Coaching helps nurses stretch and grow in order to fulfill the obligations and challenges of their current role, which ultimately influences the bottom line. Moreover, mentoring is a more informal process without specific time limits that is more navigational and continues throughout the relationship with the mentor. These techniques have become accepted and effective strategies used in the development of individuals and teams, at all levels of the organization.

Coaching and mentoring are used in nursing in a variety of ways to help nurses be the best they can be, as well as prevent problems before they occur. Coaching and mentoring help nurses to achieve professional excellence through improving leadership effectiveness, succession planning and addressing issues or concerns such as disciplinary action or accountability matters. An assumption in the coaching process is that behavioral changes will occur over time. The coaching process can reveal how the mental and emotional reactions of the nurse can interfere with personal effectiveness, performance, and well-being, as well as patient outcomes.

The need for coaching arises from an assessment through observation, and/or feedback. The feedback can come from a variety of sources including, but not limited to: peers, supervisors, patients and their families.

Tips:

- Coaching and mentoring are effective techniques for both high and low performers
- Coaching is not therapy and differs in focus, orientation, and locus of power
- Check the credentials, experience, and expertise of your prospective coach
- Coaching is based on establishing a trusting relationship between the coach and you
- Clarify upfront with your coach what information may/will be shared with key members of the organization
- It is important to select a coach that you feel comfortable with, enough to share confidential information
- The coach is generally not your direct supervisor
- Coaching focuses on the present and future, and is linked to an issue(s) that you face in your current role within the organization
- Develop SMART (specific, measurable, attainable, relevant, time-bound) goals for your coaching sessions (Doran, 1981)
- Having preconceived ideas about the opportunities for your development by the coach or yourself can lead to a negative outcome
- Coaches generally meet with the individual at their place of employment and meeting times can vary

Exercise:

Reflect on the leadership and/or other demands of your current role. Consider the areas where you believe that you would benefit from coaching or mentoring to develop the tools and strategies, or have as-needed support.

Chapter 19: In the News

Historically, nurses have been the unsung heroes who have stayed in the background, playing the supporting role. This is not the case anymore. Nurses are now at the forefront of developing, implementing, and leading healthcare change. More and more they are being recognized for their valuable contribution, and we are seeing nurses in the spotlight in a variety of media venues; such as television, radio, written articles, and social media, to name a few. Whenever you are recognized or acknowledged, it is recommended that you keep a copy of the print material or a copy of the link to the media for your professional portfolio and for your files. This is an important part of your career story and having a copy of the print material or media can be used to substantiate and support your credibility, your expertise, and also help you market yourself for successful results.

Tips:

- A soon as you have been mentioned "In the News," place a copy in your portfolio or identified file

Exercise:

Go back and retrospectively retain a copy of the print or electronic files where you were recognized.

Chapter 20: Strategies for a Successful Career Journey

You are now familiar with the twenty components of the Professional Development Toolkit to help you better articulate your strengths, skills, talents and abilities as you navigate your career. You are now prepared with the tools and the resources for self-promotion to meet the challenges to explore, lead, and create a strategic vision for growth and sustainability in today's healthcare environment. The twenty components of the Professional Development Toolkit will assist you with your ongoing professional and personal development, and assist you with marketing strategies and techniques to achieve successful results.

As you proceed along the path of your career, here are a few final tips for success.
- Welcome the challenging events in your life and think of them as opportunities to stretch and grow
- Celebrate your accomplishments and achievements, and those of your colleagues and peers
- Own what belongs to you, and don't assume responsibility for that which you have no authority over
- Be quick to listen, slow to speak and slow to react
- Network, network, network
- Assemble an informal advisory board and meet with them regularly, in good times and in bad
- Know your strengths, skills, talents, and abilities and market yourself continuously
- Be creative and innovative, and tap into your entrepreneurial spirit frequently and regularly
- Remain true to your passions and be motivated by your dream for success rather than your fear of failure
- Realize that failure is nothing more than the opportunity to pause and rethink direction (Smith, 2008)

Most importantly remember...developing *professionally* is a *lifelong journey* and the best investment is in YOU! So go forth and do the GREAT things you were created for, and were always capable of doing.

References

Advanced Research Systems, (2011). Health care background screening is of critical importance. Retrieved from http://www.arsbackgrounds.com/health_care_background_scree ning

Alter Group, (2011). RN turnover costs hospitals an estimated $9.75 billion annually. Retrieved from http://www.altergroup.com/alter-care-blog/index.php/healthcare/rn-turnover-costs/

American Association of Colleges of Nursing, (2011). Nursing fact sheet. Retrieved from http://www.aacn.nche.edu/media-relations/fact-sheets/nursing-fact-sheet

American Nurses Association, Nursing World, (2010). Code of ethics for nurses with interpretive statements. Retrieved from http://www.nursingworld.org/codeofethics

American Nurses Association, Nursing World, (2011). Fact sheet: Navigating the world of social media. Retrieved from http://www.nursingworld.org/FunctionalMenuCategories/About ANA/Social-Media/Social-Networking-Principles-Toolkit/Fact-Sheet-Navigating-the-World-of-Social-Media.pdf

CBSNEWS.com, (2013). Angel of death, part one. *60 Minutes.* Retrieved from http://www.cbsnews.com/videos/angel-of-death-part-one-2/

CBSNEWS.com, (2013). Angel of death, part two. *60 Minutes.* Retrieved from http://www.cbsnews.com/videos/angel-of-death-part-two/

Chambers, P. D. (2010). Tap the unique strengths of the millennial generation. *Nursing2010, February, 40*(2):48-51. doi: 10.1097/01.NURSE.0000367866.20941.2b.

Doran, G. T. (1981). There's a S.M.A.R.T. way to write management's goals and objectives. *Management Review, 70*(11), 35-36.

Doyle, A. (2014). How to dress for an interview: Dress code for job interviews. *About.com.* Retrieved from http://jobsearchtech.about.com/od/interviewtips/a/interview_dre ss.htm

Doyle, A., (2014). What are talent assessments and how do companies use them? *About.com.*
http://jobsearch.about.com/od/careertests/f/talentassessment.htm

Federal Trade Commission (2013). Employment background checks. Retrieved from http://www.consumer.ftc.gov/articles/0157-employment-background-checks

Gallup, (2014). Honesty/Ethics in professions. Retrieved from http://www.gallup.com/poll/1654/honesty-ethics-professions.aspx

Gorman, C. K., (2011). Seven seconds to make a first impression. *Forbes.* Retrieved from http://www.forbes.com/sites/carolkinseygoman/2011/02/13/seven-seconds-to-make-a-first-impression/

Incredible @ rt Department, (n.d.). Color symbolism chart. Retrieved from http://www.incredibleart.org/lessons/middle/color2.htm

Institute of Medicine (2011). The future of nursing: Leading change, advancing health. Washington, DC: The National Academies Press.

Joint Commission (2012). Requirements for Criminal Background Checks. Retrieved from http://www.jointcommission.org/mobile/standards_information/jcfaqdetails.aspx?StandardsFAQId=258&StandardsFAQChapterId=66

Kurtz, A. (2013). For nursing jobs, new grads need not apply. *CNN Money.* Retrieved from http://money.cnn.com/2013/01/14/news/economy/nursing-jobs-new-grads/

MacKusick, C. I. & Minick, P. (2010). Why are nurses leaving? Findings from an initial qualitative study on nursing attrition. *MEDSURG Nursing, November/December, 19*(6), 335-340.

Mercer, M., (2014). Pre-employment tests. Retrieved from http://www.mercersystems.com/pre-employmenttesting.html

Merriam-Webster, Incorporated, (2014). Validity. Retrieved from http://www.merriam-webster.com/concise/validity

Merriam-Webster, Incorporated, (2014). Reliability. Retrieved from http://www.merriam-webster.com/dictionary/reliability

National Student Nurses' Association, Inc., (n.d.). Recommendations for: Social media usage and maintaining privacy, confidentiality

and professionalism. Retrieved from
http://www.nsna.org/Portals/0/Skins/NSNA/pdf/NSNA_Social_
Media_Recommendations.pdf

Riegel, D. G., (2013). The problem with your elevator pitch--and how
to fix it. *Fast Company*. Retrieved from
http://www.fastcompany.com/3004484/problem-your-elevator-
pitch-and-how-fix-it

Wood, C., (April/2011). Employment in health care: A crutch for the
ailing economy during the 2007–09 recession. *Monthly Labor
Review*. Retrieved from
http://www.bls.gov/opub/mlr/2011/04/art2full.pdf